Based on a true story

Copyright © 2017 by Geoff Schmidt

All rights reserved. This book or any portion thereof may not be reproduced or used in any manner whatsoever without the express written permission of the publisher except for the use of brief quotations in a book review.

Printed in the United States of America

First Printing, 2017

ISBN-13:
978-1974432844

ISBN-10:
197443284X

www.schmillustrator.weebly.com

schmillustrator@gmail.com

THE ART TEACHER IS WEIRD

written and illustrated by Geoff Schmidt

Cincinnati, Ohio

Have you seen our new art teacher?
He's strange to say the least
I haven't met him personally
But the other kids call him "Beast"

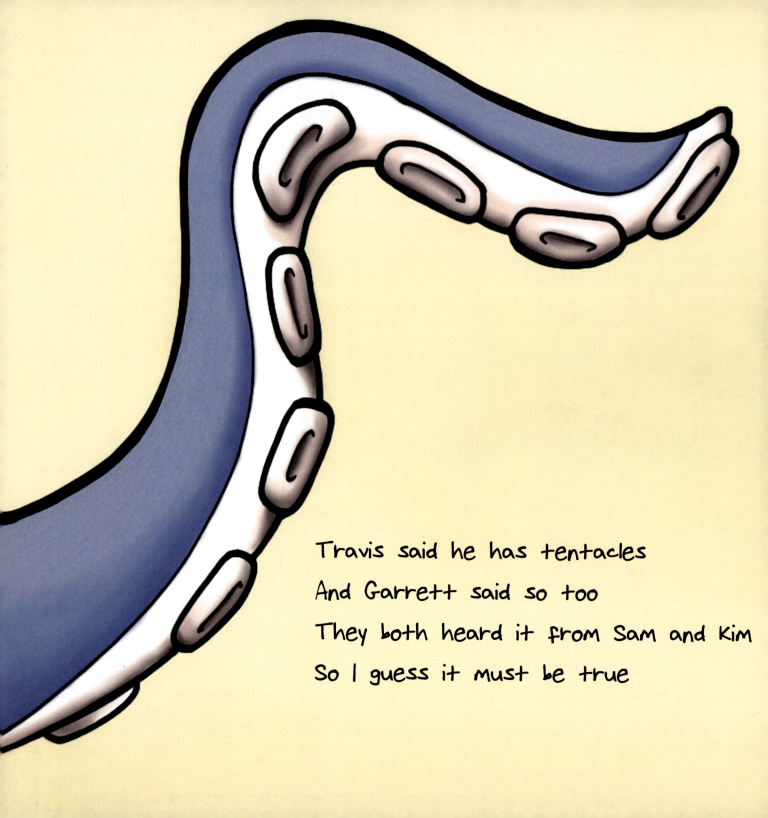

Travis said he has tentacles
And Garrett said so too
They both heard it from Sam and Kim
So I guess it must be true

Margaret said his teeth are huge
As sharp as she's ever seen
Angel said he has a yellow tongue
Squirming about in between

Carly tried to sneak a peek
Through the window in the door
She said she thought he might be blue
But she couldn't be totally sure

Teri told me he has big horns
They grow right out of his head

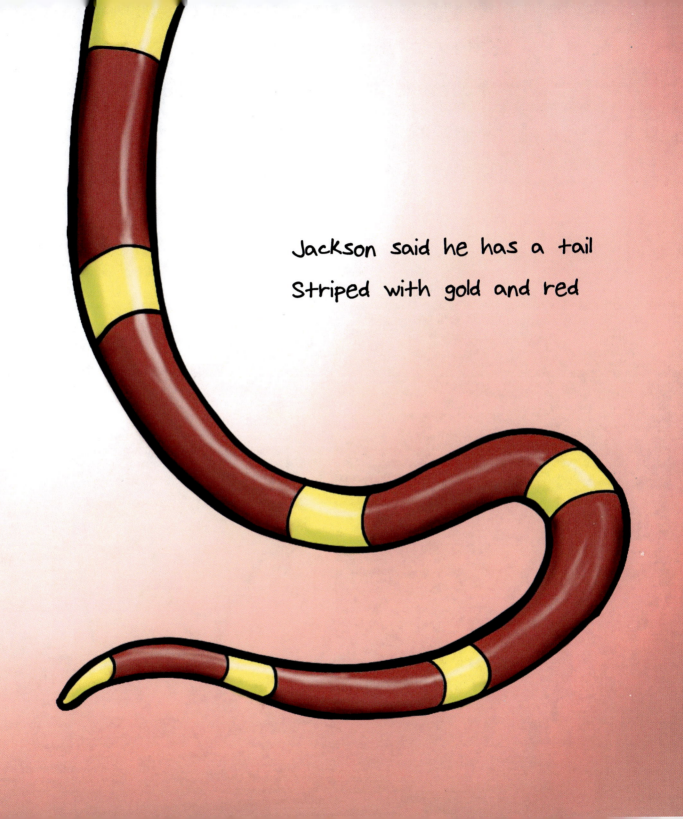

Jackson said he has a tail
Striped with gold and red

Betty swore he was an alien
Who came from beyond the stars
As proof she shared this photo
Of him jumping around on Mars

It's possible he's a monster
And a very odd one no lie
To pretend he's one of us
He always rocks a tie

I finally got to meet him
On my very first day of Art
I have to say it's a lot of things
That set this guy apart

He's got two big horns and a tail
And his skin's as blue as the sky
Can he really be our teacher?
I just can't believe my eyes

He sculpts with his tail

And keeps paint up his nose

He could walk around the room
But he chooses to dance instead

If you're paying close attention
To his face each time he speaks
You'll see his eyes get wider
And different colors in his cheeks

I used to think Mrs. Diddle was the weirdest teacher in town

And really she probably was
Until this one came around

He truly is as strange
As all the other kids say
But still he comes to school
Each and every day

Geoff Schmidt is an elementary art teacher who has also written these books:

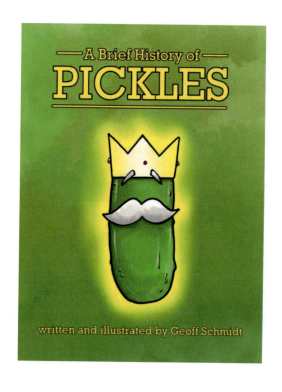

A Brief History of Pickles

The Schmillustrator's Coloring Book

Currently available on Amazon

Made in the USA
Middletown, DE
08 September 2023